THE HEART OF A MAN

BY RANDY SANCHEZ

In dedication to my parents
Nelson Sanchez
&
Dominga Estevez

TABLE OF CONTENTS

1. Love Paradise . . . . pg. 6
2. Lost in Paradise . . . . pg. 8
3. Fervid . . . . pg. 10
4. Ghost . . . . pg. 12
5. The Demon of My Nightmares . . . . . pg. 15
6. Her . . . . pg. 18
7. This is War . . . . pg. 21
8. String Theory . . . . pg. 23
9. My Cinderella . . . . pg. 25
10. The Garden of Eden . . . . pg. 27
11. PTSD . . . . pg. 29
12. The Untold Truth . . . . pg. 31
13. Insatiable Thirst . . . . pg. 33
14. Lock Heart . . . . pg. 35
15. Ecstasy . . . . pg. 37
16. Steal Your Night . . . . pg. 39
17. The Art of Redemption . . . . pg. 41

18. Ecstasy Pt. II . . . . pg. 44

19. Independence Day . . . . pg. 46

20. Epilogue - Lion Heart . . . . pg. 50

Love Paradise

Stuck on an island,
Nowhere to go,
All I can do: survive.
Stranded, but this island,
Is where everything was meant to be.
Peaceful, safe, and beautiful.
Just how it is, in your arms.
Now just imagine us
On this island,
Escaped from the world.
We settled for the white sand,
Cold drinks, blue ocean,
Pure sky, and clean air.
Where the coconut trees give the best shade,
Where nothing could make this moment better,
Where peace lives within us.
We'd watch the sun rise and set
Upon our skin,
When day rises, all we admire is each other's company,
And when night falls,
We blanket each other's bodies,
Let the stars light the night,
And our love glows stronger than the moon.
A permanent vacation,
How lovely would that be?
A world where we can live at ease,
Let the water wash away our sins
As our toes play with the sand below.
Drink from the refreshing tree of life,

To keep us young and alive.
An eternity with you,
Is a dream come true,
And this island we live on
Is far beyond comprehension.
All that matters is your smile,
How it accelerates my heart,
Yet keeps me calm.
How your laugh,
Makes me blush,
How your kisses,
Give me goosebumps,
How your touch,
Makes these butterflies go wild,
And when you speak, so soft,
Everything is silent,
And my heart pounds
Out of control,
And I become weak, feeling extremely fatigued.
How you saved me from everything.
Let us set journey,
Let us escape.
Let our love live free and wild
Where everything is perfect,
Just Like you.
Perfect.
Let's go to the best place in the world,
Just us.
Me and you, my love.
Let us set journey to -
Love Paradise.

Lost in Paradise

It's beyond an addiction,
The taste of your lips,
The electricity when your skin touches mine.
Let's not start with those eyes;
That's how it all starts: the eyes.
I'll drift to a paradise where only I live, in complete peace and harmony.
The desire to be here never leaves, but it feels like the days are becoming gloomy, grey.
Food never loses its taste, but the essence of eating has.
Now this paradise doesn't seem so green anymore, Just quiet. Extremely quiet.
The hypnotic motion of your eyes put me in a state where I was complete.
Things were beyond perfect,
But little by little, I learned hypnosis only worked on me.
Stranded on an island, full, but alone.
I set journey to find answers to why,
Why am I the only one here?
Don't you want to experience this with me?
Be my peace and I be yours?
Maybe the reason I'm stranded here is to understand, but you never wanted that.
Maybe you don't know how to express it back.

Late, as the ocean crashes against the night,
The air becomes crisp and it is easier to close my eyes.

But I can't fall asleep, alone in the cold.
All I can think of is you.
Wishing you'd come save me from this hellhole.
Constantly writing S.O.S on the sand, hoping you'd find it.
All I could find was the ocean.
All I could do was think of you,
Wondering where you are,
wishing you'd hear me, you'd feel my cries,
You'd save my day.
That's what it was - I wanted to be saved, but I wanted it to be you.
But you didn't want to save me.
Where are those that save the ones who do the saving?
We were a team, right?
Us against the world, right?
Now it's just me,
Lost in Paradise

Fervid

I never knew
Such animality could live within me.
In your presence,
I became a new man.
How interesting,
That the nerves in my body begin to startle
When my fingertips tremble across your skin.
Oh,
How I lose my breath when I have you so close to me,
I can no longer stand before you, my Queen.
Why do I deserve to stand face to face with a Queen like you.
The only Queen that ever existed.
A true Goddess.
Indeed, what I say is true.
For a man like I
To sacrifice it all,
To witness you, in the flesh.
This must be my luckiest day.
I fear you, my Queen.
I will devote my life to your service,
And worship your smile.
Oh, how it completes my life
To see you,
Happy as the fairytales,
Your existence is unfathomable,
But look at you, in the flesh.
And now I am at your service, my Queen.
An insolent human like I,

Cannot compare to someone like you;
Someone far beyond perfection.
But I never knew,
This animal would live within me
When your presence is near.
Pumping in my heart,
The beast calls out to you.
I have striven for this,
To stand next to you, my Queen.
When I do, I become a new man.
How interesting it is,
When the nerves in my body begin to spark,
When my fingertips tremble across your skin,
Oh, I must say,
How I lose my breath when I have you so close to me,
I can no longer stand before you, my Queen.
How can I deserve to stand face to face with a Queen like you.
You are absolute perfection;
And this animal within me,
Is just the man I am.
And I cannot help but fall
Continuously for you, my Queen.
You are the owner of my heart,
I will stand by your side until the very end.
Even if you are the world's our greatest enemy,
I will still be your knight.
We shall name the beast within me:
Fervid

Ghost

Welcome to reality,
A world where we all co-exist
A world full of pain, rage, insanity, and selfishness.
Yet, through all of that,
We can still find magic,
We call it love -
An escape from reality.
We all question our place here,
Hoping to one day make a statement
To the world, or just to ourselves.
Even in this reality,
I'm trapped in the nether-realm,
A world filled with darkness,
Alone.
Where my tears cannot be seen,
Where my voice can't be heard,
Where I will decay.
As a child, I was always the fool.
Behind the whole world,
When all I wanted was to be a part of this world.
Always chosen last
Always ignored
Always pitied.
I asked myself,
Who am I?
Why do I exist?
Do I exist?
As time went on, it constantly felt like I didn't.
I was just a shadow to those with pretty faces,
Those with facades of a good heart.

Easily, brushing you off;
And all I wanted was to love.
To escape into another world with you.
My love, this world hurts.
And in total darkness,
I ask,
Who am I?
Why do I exist?
Do I exist?
I imagined my touching your face,
Finally being loved.
Noticed for the man I am.
Because these tears burn,
And my heart bleeds eternally.
I want you to make me feel human,
I don't want to live in this cold dark world.
You are the only one,
My escape from reality.
I plead, I scream, I cry;
For you to hear me.
When the demons are always laughing in the back of my head.
I just wish for you to wash it all away,
Maybe one day,
Maybe.
But as child,
I was a shadow,
Behind those facades.
I am human, invisible to reality,
Always pitied,
Always chosen last,
Always ignored,

I just want to be noticed, by You;
I exist, but yet; in reality, I didn't.
I'm just a nobody,
Wanting to be a somebody,
I am
Ghost

The Demon of My Nightmares

Thump thump
Shh, do you hear that?
Thump thump
How it pounds deeply,
Crying away, screaming so loud.
Hoping others can hear it,
Thump thump
Signals are being sent to the brain,
Trying to find a way to escape the darkness.
How fearsome it is, to be in hell's bound.
Thump thump
Now all I wish is to go home.
The mosh pit of bodies,
And stench of the man that we all fear,
Death.
Thump thump
I can remember your faces,
Your demonic faces,
Thump thump
The monsters that would be the fear of our fears.
True hypnotism, I must say.
Where your dreams are actual nightmares,
And your heart is scared of your mind.
Thump thump
And your mind is petrified to how your heart would react,
Thump thump
But at night, I may feel at ease,
I am indeed screaming for your help;
Thump thump

When I saw your demonic face,
Oh, you demon from hell,
Why have you come to torture me?
Thump thump
You are my fear's fear,
My ally, but then again,
Thump thump
My enemy;
And who is this I speak of?
Well of the course the heaven itself,
When a Goddess like you comes to exist,
I couldn't help but fall in love.
Thump thump
Because you became the reason I can dream,
Thump thump
But you are also my nightmares,
Thump thump
When my dreams were real, I never wanted to rest,
And my nightmares were when your presence wasn't near.
Thump thump
Oh, how you manipulated the factors of my senses,
Thump thump
You demon!
Thump thump
How madly in love I am with you,
Thump thump
This is just another of your hell-bound tricks to follow you into the pits of darkness,
Thump thump
And yet, you are so delicate & warm.
You put me at ease,

Thump thump
Sacrificing the fall,
To make it worth it all,
Thump thump
A dream that is truly a nightmare,
Thump thump
She is
Thump thump
The Demon of My Nightmare

Her

I've written about you,
You know?
All from the dreams that I had as a child.
These stories that I created as I daydreamed my
childhood away.
Astonishing really,
That one can exist through a character in a dream.
The Dream Girl,
The woman I have dreamt of since birth.
Oh, you amaze me every time.
When I gaze upon you and your beautiful smile,
Distant, but I feel it deep within me.
I become a foolish child
When I'm around you -
Uncontrollably nervous,
Giggling - I can't stop smiling
When I have such beauty near me.
Words cannot connect with my tongue.

Enough of this,
I've spent so much time,
Learning the person I dreamt of.
How outstanding it is
When moments get quiet
I can hear your voice call out to my heart,
"Don't leave," as if I wanted to be anywhere else.
And when the night came,
Your body wrapped around mine,
Making sure you would be safe as you slept,

And I made sure that even in your dreams, I would be your superman.
That's when you asked me,
"What is your fear?"
My kryptonite: *You.*
When your caring voice gives me warmth,
When your touch gives me butterflies,
When you drive me crazy.
I am terrified of losing you,
Someone using you, treating you as a tool
To hurt me, to hurt you,
To hurt the world.
But I learned to be with
Someone who is as outstanding,
Intelligent, talented, persistent, as you,
So that at the end of the day,
We can lie back,
And you can whisper in my ears,
"Everything is okay; there is nothing to worry about."
Although the world is falling,
You're all I have, and I don't want to lose you.
So this Dream Girl,
She exists,
She is you.
And now I spend every day looking forward to making your heart smile.
I build my life in order to live it with you.
Because no matter where I go,
There is nothing better than coming home to you,
My love.

So let us carve the story that is left in our novels, together.
I will risk it all, to be right here beside you.
You're all I've got;
All I ever wanted.
All I need.
Together, we will change the world.
We'll show that dreams do come true,
Together, forever.
This is something my heart has dreamt of and will continue to fight for,
For eternity.
I give you my heart, my love.
I give you my all.

This is in dedication to
Her

This is War

I fell in love with the Devil.
I thought that things were just unfolding.
It turns out the devil disguises itself as what you most desire -
For me, a best friend.
Demons danced around as I fell in love.
Dancing with the Devil
As I try to shake them off, one by one.
Deep inside my mind, I laid the leftover ammunition for them to come right back,
Haunting me once more.
The thing is, I always look to brighten your day,
Fight to make you smile,
Do the best I could, so I could have you in my arms.
I was never enough.
When I lied in bed, there was a knife right behind me.
The same knife I used to defend myself.
The same knife I used to carve your name into my skin.
And now it can never be erased from my soul.
You left, and these demons just torment me.

I danced with the Devil, and was left to burn in hell.

All I ever wanted was a best friend. You.
I wanted to quit, but the rage wouldn't let me.
I wanted to scream, but the rage wouldn't let me.
I wanted to cry, but the rage wouldn't let me.

And of course I'm sad, these wounds can still feel the sting,
The stitches are still opening.
But this rage, this rage feels like lava.
Boiling, burning.
These demons,
This Devil,
These burnt marks,
They will all come to an end,
And I don't want to stop.
I don't want to be a useless, pathetic coward,
Just like how you let those demons insult me,
Over and over, telling me those words would "help me improve."
I don't know if I'm ready and I don't care.
I will stand strong on my feet,
Show you what I'm truly made of.
I will not quit, ever.

This is War

String Theory

My pen is running out of ink,
Constantly writing to you,
Describing you, helping me fall more and more for you.
As the ink expresses your beauty, solid and a known fact on paper.
The scripture of your beauty slowly takes shape.
Now, it's hard to write a love letter,
It's hard to express my love,
To make the effort to see that smile.
But I have this theory:
Have you ever dreamt of something
That becomes reality?
How is that so?
Universes and universes,
Endless time, where life is born, and of course, ends.
An infinite opportunity of possibilities.
Now the reason I mention this is because
Of all the things that exist,
That one thing that you have imagined,
Wished upon,
Happens to exist.
Don't call me crazy just yet,
This heart may know no sanity,
But look at you,
Shining brighter than any star.
Your presence shifts when you enter the room,
Your soul, enticing, it's warm and bright.
It feels as if it gives me the energy to continue on,

Even when I want to give up.
You believe in me, and that smile makes it worth it, every time.
That smile - so mesmerizing,
Those lips, rosy, dying to taste their endless wonder.
Now,
I have always believed in the theory of infinite possibility,
So what are the odds
That the person of my dreams,
Is standing before me.
I call this:
String Theory

My Cinderella

I can't help but to look at you.
"What? Do I have something on my face?"
Yes, and it's remarkable.
I can't imagine how something could be created in such a way
That it will always take my breath away.
How do you do that?
I want to learn everything about you,
Admire you as you glow,
As you grow,
As you improve,
And as you turn, smile, and know
That I'll always be there beside you.
There is nothing you must ever worry about,
Because there is nothing out there
That will be as outstanding as you.
Nothing has ever been too hard of a challenge,
You make it look so easy -
Being flawless, being you.
Never have I said there won't be challenges that will make you struggle,
But even then;
Flawlessly, you awe the world.
God, you are so perfect.
And don't tell me you're not, that kills me inside.
You don't have to be perfect for the world,
But you are perfect to me.
I must ask, do you believe in destiny?
I was placed here to meet something so magnificent - I call that pure luck.

You managed to take my breath away,
And I still find it hard to believe.
But I love it, how you just glow.
I would love to stand there every day next to you,
Watching you smile, watching you glow.
I can admire you all day long.
God, you are so perfect.
My Cinderella

The Garden of Eden

I didn't think you'd ever exist,
A myth,
We would just create our own image of you,
It's what made us feel whole.
Safe, comfortable.
In such a dark place we live in,
Things have never felt any brighter.
It feels like a spiritual getaway.
Here's the thing,
I came across you because of pure luck.
Upon a journey on finding myself,
...Or maybe just to recollect my mind.
I came across you,
Fascinated, shocked, in awe.
Truly breathtaking.
I wish I could stay here forever,
But it's not always going to be so green.
And here's the other thing,
Being here showed me.
Helped me reminisce,
Helped me forget,
Helped me break,
Helped me build.
Through the stories,
Through the tears,
Through the stars that shined in the night,
Through the fact that I believed in my journey,
I felt like I was spiraling to my own doom,
Losing myself,
Hoping that I would be saved.

Hoping you would see me.
But you showed me
The attention that I was seeking wasn't what I needed.
You showed me your beauty
To help mine flourish.
Now I stand on my feet,
Not asking to be saved or seen.
You showed me to be myself,
And nothing is greener than that.
Thank you for this experience.
The world may be a dark place,
But it is I who must keep the darkness out.
This journey is just beginning.
I never knew that a myth
Would help me remember who I am.
You brought me back to this world.
Thank You,
La Isla Quisqueya,
As the legends once called it.
The Garden of Eden

PTSD

The memories no longer let me sleep,
I thought there would come a day I thought I would be safe
From you,
My prized possession became my worst nightmare.
How you torment me.
Little did I know this would be harder than I could imagine.
And now it all feels as if
I was just talking to a wall, *maybe I was the whole time.*
Just like when you give a child an unconnected controller,
He thinks he's in control - that he has what it takes to beat any challenge ahead,
He lets his dreams run wild.
But we both played.
And just like that, life moved on.
I thought I had escaped these demons,
But truth be told, they will always come back.
Feeding into your mind, intoxicating your thoughts.
In the depths of night, where time stands still.
You can see them grin, and their evil eyes glow over you while you sleep.
And you just lay in bed, watching them torment you.
Can't scream, can't run,
Suffering in fear.
As time slows, you can hear your heart pound.
THUMP THUMP!
It's only a matter of time, then poof.

Either your mind breaks, or snaps.
All I can see is this menacing smile as it holds you dear.
Memories flash when the sun would creep in
as I turned to you.
I could feel your skin, soft as silk.
You had this glow in your eyes that made it worthwhile to be alive.
It was you who gave me the strength to fight until the end of time.
I never knew tomorrow.
I never knew that tomorrow
You'd be dancing with the devil.
It was just yesterday that I had you wrapped in my arms,
Now, these demons haunt me.
I wonder if you have your own; *maybe I'm one of them.*
Maybe dancing with me was your devil,
And you've moved on to the next show.
Now I sit in quarantine,
Trying to relinquish this
Post-Traumatic Stress Disorder

The Untold Truth

Journal Entry,
Time has passed since my mind broke,
But this time I'm taking a moment to just speak.
Maybe to myself, maybe to the world,
Inside of my head...I really don't care who listens,
But it is nice to be heard.
The things I want to say are just...feelings.
The thing is, I've been lost.
Focusing on myself, searching for something to replace,
Maybe that's the right way to say it.
Maybe it's that I hate the silence between the four walls that I confine myself in.
I no longer need to cry, scream.
I eat just fine, and I sleep at night.
But the thought never stops running through my head.
Maybe I'm just not meant to be for you,
And that's just a hard fact to live with,
Because nobody can do what I can do,
And all I want
Is to see you smile.
I watched you sell your soul to the devil,
And that worries me.
But who am I? Just a lost mind.
I will never understand, only try to.
Time and time again, I feel myself drifting apart from my own reality,
Looking for something to complete me.
I thought I could fill this void with your affection,

But...that was never the case.
I try too hard, I love too hard, and I forgive too easily.
So, this data entry is to remind me
To never lose track.
The devil still lingers and wishes to burn me in hell.
I need to fix myself, I need to be strong.
Hopefully, too strong.
So that I can be who I am,
Without chains pulling me down.
Set my tunnel vision towards who I need to be.
To one day make you proud.
Better yet, make myself proud.
I was losing my touch,
I thought I was losing my mind, thought that I wasn't playing my chess pieces correctly.
It's time to take a step back,
Breathe and go for it.
Focus.
The fear of wanting to shift my attention to this void shall be nevermore.
I can't keep somebody content, if I am not content within.
I keep trying so hard
To put a smile on your face
And I forgot how to make myself happy.
Entry Complete
The Untold Truth

Insatiable Thirst

Something inside of my head
Keeps playing over and over again
Driving me crazy, yet, it's satisfying.
That smile of yours,
I just let it go.
I feel so drawn to it,
I want to see it all the time.
Is that crazy?
I can't forget it—the taste of you still lingers on my tongue.
I can feel it, feel your lips pressed against mine.
They taste like mango,
Like sweet chocolate,
Like baked bread fresh from the oven.
And now I crave you,
The way your skin is so soft, so pure.
Maybe I'm delusional, but when you carved your fingernails into my back,
The intensity burned with such desire.
And that's all I can think of,
Making your desires become reality,
Learning all your deepest secrets.
Maybe I have figured it out, just…maybe.
It's the essence of your presence.
An early Sunday morning, summer time all the time.
And when I get a taste of that hot brewed coffee,
It's like it was made from the grains of richest beans
In the entire universe.

So pure, strong, delicious, powerful.
I feel like I could rule the world.
Yet, I just want to rule yours.
Summer days,
With the taste of your fruitful lips,
Make you feel like your dreams are nothing compared to what I do.
Feed your desires, as your toes curl back.
Winter nights,
Engrave my name into your skin,
Create electricity as our bodies touch,
Wrap you in my arms, so you can feel safe.
Make your dreams run wild.
It's only you,
I can't explain it.
I just want to see you smile,
I can't help myself.
The way you bite your lips, the fire in your eyes when you look at me.
The tone in your voice when you speak to me,
And the smile that started it all.
I know you can feel this
Insatiable Thirst

Lock Heart

I never thought I'd see you again,
Maybe it's the fact that I didn't think about it as much.
I didn't know if I would ever hear from you,
I finally began to believe you were dead
...And nobody comes back from there.
But here you are, a ghost.
Maybe it's an illusion,
My mind playing tricks hoping that you do miss me,
I may never know, I don't really know.
But it felt strange,
I <u>don't</u> want it to be you;
So I keep hoping it isn't.
You knew you had my heart wrapped around your finger.
You knew I lost myself while making you happy.
You knew we needed time apart.
But I didn't know that I was the only one who was able to understand you.
And you didn't know that I have your heart locked deep within you;
It can't be touched the way that I did.
Our memories became the foundation of what it is,
The imprint of my power gives you goosebumps.
Now you crave the cure to your curse.
You think there is someone out there,
But it's only me.
You are chained, and I guess you reached out like a poltergeist
To tell me so.

Maybe after some time you thought another chance would be better.
Maybe now is the right moment.
It took me a few days to realize
That the way I made you feel
Is the way I feel now, without you:
Unstoppable.
Just the rush, knowing that
Nobody can love you like I can.
I had a lot of love to give, and you weren't the one to give it to.
Knowing that,
I still have the key
To your
Lock Heart

Ecstasy

I didn't know you would be wonderful
From head to toe,
Endless sensation.
From the sudden breaths you take,
To the way you scream.
The tension you bring upon me
Writing an endless love song
Show you the world through me,
As I admire you,
from that smile, to your eyes—
How it glows in the light.
The words you express yourself with,
The beliefs that you hold so dear.
It's impossible to think you are a masterpiece—
A work of art I've never seen before.
And when the night comes,
I'll polish you in every way possible.
Show you that your demons are mine to tame.
The one that makes you lose control.
Give in to my hunger,
Let me show you the masterpiece you are.
An endless sensation,
You can feel it make your legs tremble.
You can feel it as your eyes roll back.
Your sweat tastes so good.
An insatiable thirst to show you far beyond this world.
Let me show you energy beyond comprehension.
Something only you and I will understand.

Nobody will do the things that I can.
I'll make your wildest fantasies come true
All just to see you smile.
Show you the thrill of
Ecstasy

Steal Your Night

I've learned to stop overthinking things,
But sometimes I just can't help it.
When you are in control of certain situations,
You may overanalyze how things should play out,
Intelligence can be counterintuitive,
It can drive you to the brink of insanity.
I kept questioning myself,
I couldn't stop thinking, *are these the right moves?*
Am I right for you?
And as the night went on,
The bachata played,
Creating the essence of life.
It was the art of passion that helped me build the courage to ask for a dance.
The music everyone studies so hard to learn and appreciate.
But I use this art to study you and your perfection.
The night moves swiftly,
Time feels irrelevant,
And all I can see is the glow in your eyes.
Four steps to the left,
Four steps to the right,
In perfect rhythm.
As I hold your hand with one, and press your waist against me with the other,
I can feel your radiance.
You caress me and hold me tight.
Inside I'm driven wild by the allure of your sweet scent.
Time no longer feels relevant with you,

All I see is you,
Taking the night away.
And as time goes on, we grow closer and closer.
You wrap your fingers around the back of my neck and press me once more.
I can feel your spirit burning with every step we take.
Let's take a step back, gather our thoughts.
I'm thinking too much,
It's just a dance.
But you never let go, and neither do I.
Now my soul is bound to you,
Waiting for one more dance,
Just one more dance to
Steal Your Night Away

The Art of Redemption

I can see you,
The way you smile, it's disgusting.
You wish to see me burn in hell.
The flames are as hot as the sun,
Millions of degrees.
The tension rises,
Putting nothing but challenges in front of me.
Never would I have thought you'd be my biggest enemy.
The thoughts inside my head tell me to give in.
The pleasure of letting you win
Makes me want to fight even more.
I feel so confused, so lost,
Maybe even crazy, insane possibly.
You disguised yourself as my biggest desire.
Gorgeous, almost flawless to me.
Now you want me to believe somebody else can do the things I was able to do and more.
But I was the one who carved your soul,
I molded your hands to overcome any possibility.
Truthfully, I am happy for you,
Tackling the world by a force nobody will ever understand.
You are unstoppable.
But you're greedy.
Narcissistic - you want me to be your toy,
Living in hell as you escape to the heavens,
To the land of Eden.
I kept telling myself I needed to prove my worth.

But now I hear your demons,
They lock you in with my voice,
Telling you that you will never win,
So you seek vengeance.
You show the world a facade just to belittle me.
The world is a cruel place, and it feels like you want to bring me down with it.
You were my world,
Never would I have thought that after it fell apart,
It would come back to haunt me.
I'm just a boy trying to find his way.
I shouldn't fear something I've made.
I've made my mistakes, and I'm not proud of it.
I have failed, so now I've learned how to succeed.
You can't stop me, you never will.
Send me to hell once more, I will rise.
Challenge me, I will rise.
Mock me as you please, I will rise.
I will never be stopped.
I learned from you to accept
That you are happy,
With a facade or not.
But this is only the journey -
Something I should embrace,
Appreciate, learn from.
It's a form of repossession
To know that I am no longer in your control.
Now here you are,
A figment of my imagination
Trying to push me back into your pocket
When you know that
Nobody can ever do what I do.

So watch closely
As I teach you
Your last lesson:
The Art of Redemption

Ecstasy pt. II

The thirst remains insatiable, I can't get enough of you.
Maybe it's the fact that you make me feel invincible.
Maybe it's the fact that you are considerate - you know I exist.
I can't keep you away for too long,
I can feel my body crave you.
I can feel my heart calling out your name,
The burning sensation of your presence,
The way you give me the motivation to push forward,
To wake up and tackle the world.
I was scared, terrified.
I knew you existed, but I didn't know that you were the missing piece to solve it all.
Maybe I sound a bit crazy,
Longing to feel your lips pressed against mine.
It makes me want to run halfway across the world just to get a taste.
Even if you were at the center of a field of landmines,
I'll make my way to you,
Just to have you in my arms.
Now, the thing is…I am becoming more afraid,
Day by day, I become infatuated with you.
I can't get you out of my mind the more I learn everything about you.
All the things that make you tick, all things that make you wild,
All things that can make you mine.

Now, I have this belief about perfection,
And I'm sure you've heard it by now.
You can be perfect in my eyes, but, are you perfect...for me?
I've never experienced this before.
I've never loved like this before.
I've never felt like I was both in control, and guided.
I think about it, I dream about it,
The world drives me in circles.
Up, down, left, right, every which way.
But you keep me straight.
And to this day, that's all that matters.
Never have I ever felt this love before,
But never shall I let it go.
Today I'll wake up, and I'll tackle the world.
Tomorrow, the same.
I have you, that's all that matters.
That beautiful smile on your face.
Now I know what it means to risk it all for love.
I am yours and you are mine.
Forever and always,
Ecstasy II

Independence Day

What a strange day today is,
I honestly don't know what to think anymore,
…or even write.
My mind draws a blank.
I don't feel like doing anything,
Just wake up, lie in bed and stare at the ceiling.
I know what today is.
I Softly turn over and see the absence of what was,
A mark, an imprint of what used to be, a memory.
Now all I can do is hold it fondly,
Because the tears are now dry, but the pain still exists.
And today, it struck right where it hurts the most.
I lost motivation, lost sense of who I am, lost the dreams of feeling like I was on top of the world.
I created an imagination that you gave me a rush,
The sensation of touching your skin made me feel whole.
I know what today is
It's the day I miss you the most.
The day I dedicated my all to you.

I take a trip down memory lane,
When we took our journey far across the city,
When we first met,
The way our presence changed us and molded us.
Let's not forget: we gave each other obstacles.
We had a tough road, but we were willing to face it.
I mean, you were the only one I ever thought of spending the rest of my life with.

Crazy, huh?
We used to lie in the dark, holding each other.
Telling each other that there is no other person that can fit this balance.
So the memories flood my mind,
Today, of all days.
And I can't help but remember
The way you opened up to me, made me your personal journal.
I was astonished by how every day was a regular day, but also a new adventure.
I hated everyone that hurt you.
I guess I hated myself as well.
But now, in my personal journal, I hold the values I learned fondly.
Because today, I can't help myself.
But things happen, things change.
And the memories will always be there.
The sands of the beach will be walked by many others,
But our time will have been ours.
Our moments will always be our moments,
Like when I was told you locked lips with another.
I couldn't sleep hoping that it was a rumor.
And I must do all I can,
To see it through and appreciate it all.
The good and the bad.

I must acknowledge
That I know what today is.
It's the day I miss you the most,
When you shine the brightest,

When I place all my cards on the table to see you smile,
When the world revolves around you.
It was a celebration,
But now it feels like torture.
I can't help but think about you.
Time has passed,
And I am able to sleep better,
...You slept just fine when our worlds split.
But here I am, writing about you.
Just because today
I wonder,
Do you ever think of me?

Today comes along and I can't keep track of my work,
Food loses its taste and the picture of cordon bleu sticks to my mind.
The cognac is stale and makes the pain heavier.
Everything just feels grey.
My friends say it's all right, but I just don't want to feel this way.
Man, it hurts my heart how much I loved you.
It feels like it's playing the saddest song in the world,
Weeping and sobbing,
And all I can remember is that today, I did everything I could to spend it all with you.
Now memories are memories,
Once again,
Good or bad -
We must appreciate them all.

For today, is the day I failed myself.
But it's also the day that gave me the tools to succeed.
Thank you,
Independence Day

Epilogue

Lion Heart

Dear child,

I write this letter in hopes that one day you'll know the truth.

We haven't met yet, hopefully we will someday.

But this letter is to leave you with something,

If I'm not here, I would at least like to leave this to you.

Be good and listen to your mother;

Show respect, unconditional love,

And as my child, let the world hear your burning spirit.

The world is a cold, dark place, my child.

But never be afraid…easier said than done, right?

The paths we decide to take are of our own free will,

Whether it be a desire that is the very reason our soul burns with eternal flame.

Or it the fear that will keep us hiding in the inescapable darkness.

Do not become overwhelmed with it all,

Take a deep breath, let the pieces come together.

One step at a time.

Mistakes were made in my life, and that is fine.

You, on the other hand, will start with a clean slate.

So please hear my wisdom and take advantage.

I always had this burning feeling inside of me.

To push the world into a brighter light,

I only thought to myself: *I will show the world what I am made of.*

The need to prove my value to the world was what fueled my self esteem.

The love I gave to your mother was to prove that mine was one and only.

It's better off that I kept loving and kept striving to brighten her day.

Her voice, when I returned home from a long day, always put me at ease.

Now all I can do is carve the world for you.

Show you my burning will and pass it on to you.

I once read that the burning will I have is called the Will of Fire.

But in reality it's you, my child.

I learned that what I am made of, is incomparable to who you can become.

It's far beyond comprehension.

How blessed am I to be able to write this to you!

Knowing that I can leave something behind to carry on a legacy that nobody else can.

I tackled the world, and will continue to show my worth.

Show them that light does exist.

My Will of Fire shows me that hope can be found.

I can only thank you for that.

I no longer feel fear, understand this.

I will stand against death himself, just to be able to embrace you in my arms.

Your mother knows the fire that brought us together well.

We are mere humans, but our souls feel like lions in their den.

Rise my child.

Together we shall make the world tremble, show them our burning spirit.

I will always be beside you.

Dear child,

I write this to you because I know what kind of person you are and will be.

Past or future, I know.

You are the Will of Fire.

You are the future.

Some will call you a monster for taking on the world.

But all will understand who you are.

What your heart is made of,

A Lion Heart

Printed in the USA
CPSIA information can be obtained
at www.ICGtesting.com
LVHW041146251023
761974LV00003B/16

9 798218 156664